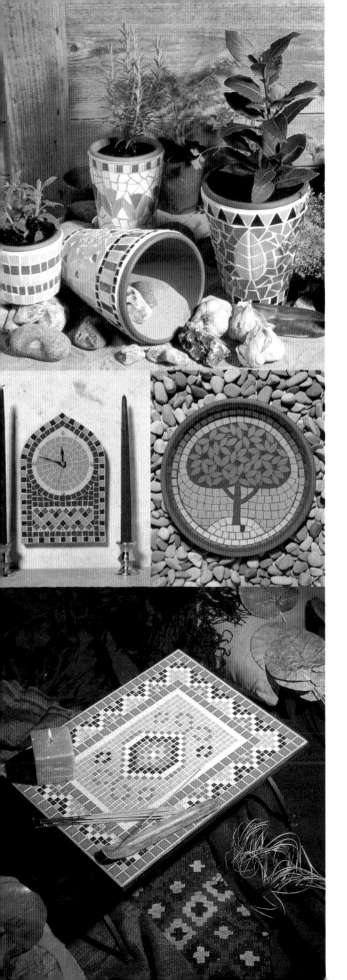

KU-315-343

Contents

Introduction   4

Materials and equipment   6

Aztec mirror frame   10
TRANSFERRING A DESIGN, GLUING AND GROUTING

Kilim table   16
CUTTING SQUARES

Seahorse panel   20
CUTTING TRIANGLES AND WEDGE SHAPES

Orange tree dish   24
CUTTING CIRCLES AND LEAF SHAPES

Jewelled clock   30
INCORPORATING BEADS AND COLOURING GROUT

Crazy plant pot   34
USING BROKEN TILES

Pepper tile   38
USING A MESH BASE

Fancy fish panel   42
INDIRECT TECHNIQUE

Index   48

Introduction

Mosaic is one of the most ancient and inventive forms of surface decoration. The term mosaic refers to the grouping together of many small elements to form a whole.

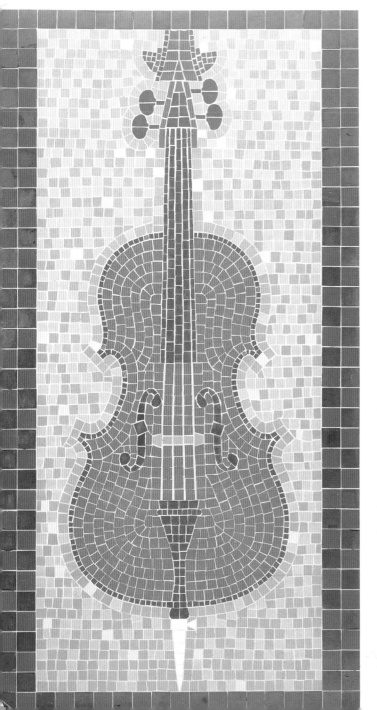

The legacy of mosaic stretches back around 5,000 years to Mesopotamia, where coloured clay pegs were arranged in geometric patterns set into mortar. Over the following centuries, successive civilisations developed the art and introduced new materials. Both aesthetic and functional, mosaic produces a resilient surface with colours that tend not to fade. As testament to this, many examples have remained intact for thousands of years.

The Greeks used large areas of small pebbles to create the first representational mosaics, many featuring their gods. Roman times saw a continuation and refinement of the techniques. Small cubes, known as *tesserae*, were cut from stone and glass. New conventions of pattern and style evolved, many of which are still in use today. Roman designs were often highly detailed and realistic. They offer a fascinating insight into all aspects of Roman life, depicting scenes such as feasting and gladiatorial combat.

During the Byzantine era, the application of glass tesserae, known as *smalti*, increased. A huge palette of vibrant colours and the extensive use of gold enabled mosaic to express extraordinary power. Visit the former Byzantine capital of Ravenna in northern Italy, to see some of the most inspiring works.

Extensive use of mosaic continued throughout the Middle Ages. Fine examples of floor, wall and ceiling mosaics can be seen at St Mark's Cathedral in Venice.

A BEGINNER'S GUIDE TO

MOSAIC

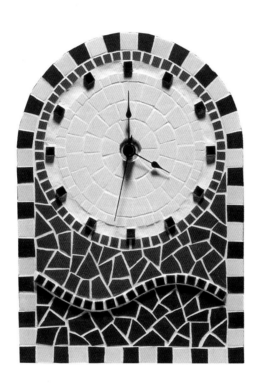

PETER MASSEY & ALISON SLATER

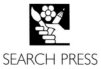

SEARCH PRESS

First published in Great Britain 1999

Search Press Limited
Wellwood, North Farm Road,
Tunbridge Wells, Kent TN2 3DR

Reprinted 2000, 2002, 2003

Suppliers
If you have difficulty in obtaining any of the materials and equipment
mentioned in this book, then please write to the Publishers at the
above address, or to Royal Sovereign requesting a list of distributers.

Royal Sovereign
7 St Georges Industrial Estate
White Hart Lane
London, N22 5QL

Colour separation by P&W Graphics, Singapore
Printed in Spain by A.G. Elkar S. Coop. 48180 Loiu (Bizkaia)

To the Taylor family

Publisher's note
All the step-by-step photographs in this book feature the
authors, Peter Massey and Alison Slater, demonstrating how to
mosaic. No models have been used.

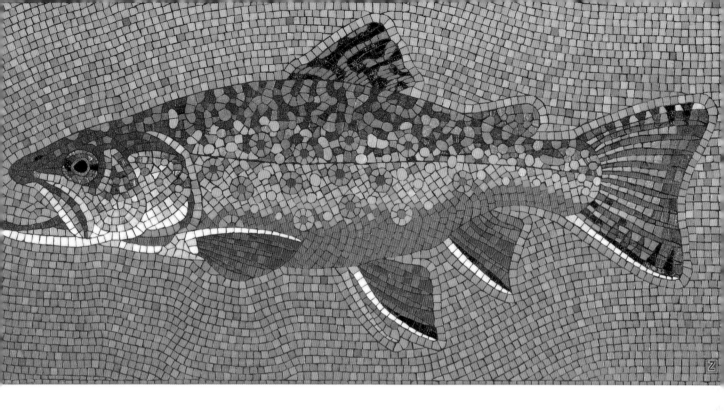

By the eighteenth century, a style of mosaic had developed which recreated the effect of oil painting. Works by artists such as Raphael were realised in mosaic to great effect. Mosaic miniatures became popular and were frequently incorporated into snuff boxes, plaques and jewellery.

The great decorative revival of the Art Nouveau movement saw a rediscovery of mosaic, with strong organic and abstract designs adorning modern public buildings such as railway stations, theatres and department stores. In Barcelona, multicoloured broken ceramic mosaic known as *trencadis* was used to cover the exterior of buildings and sculptures. This technique was made famous by modernist architects including Antoni Gaudi.

Today mosaics are a familiar sight everywhere. Twentieth-century artists have enhanced the surfaces that surround our daily modern lives. The common use of mosaic in airports, hospitals, subways and swimming pools illustrates its versatility.

The availability of inexpensive industrially-manufactured materials makes mosaic an accessible craft for those eager to try a new creative discipline. The possibilities are endless . . . from small intricate designs to large-scale works covering whole walls or floors. Its resistance to wear and tear makes it suitable for both interior and exterior applications.

This book will introduce you to the techniques unique to mosaic. Step-by-step photographs will guide you through eight projects, ranging from a simple whole-tile mirror frame to a more complex cut-tile panel.

Once you are familiar with the techniques, try creating your own designs or interpreting existing ones. This may sound a little daunting, but even the most simple geometric patterns can look fantastic when grouted and polished.

Making mosaics can be time-consuming, but it is an immensely rewarding pursuit and you will find that the hours invested are well spent.

Materials & equipment

The basic tools and materials used in mosaic-making are relatively inexpensive and easily obtainable. The list shown here is extensive, but you do not need all these items to get started. Certain tools are required for certain techniques – study the *You Will Need* section at the beginning of each project.

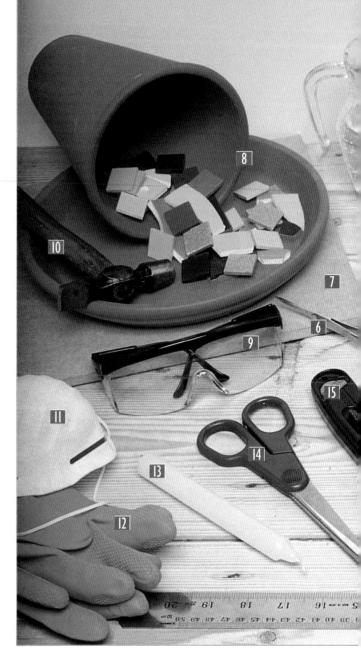

HEALTH AND SAFETY WARNING

Cutting Cutting mosaic tiles inevitably produces sharp fragments and shards. Even with experience, these have a tendency to fly off in all directions! A pair of goggles is essential to protect your eyes.

Never use your hand to remove small shards from your mosaic or work surface – always use a brush.

Grouting The wearing of goggles, rubber gloves and a dust mask is advised for all processes involving grout. Always study the manufacturer's recommendations on the packaging.

---

1. **Art Mosaic professional quality grout** This fine grade grout is specially formulated for the small gaps inherent in mosaic. There are many different grouting compounds on the market. Some, like this one, are supplied in powder form and require mixing with water, whilst others come as ready-mixed paste. Grout is available in a number of shades (although only white and terracotta grout powder are shown here). Alternatively, you may decide to colour it yourself using acrylic paint. Grouting can be a rather messy process! It is a good idea to protect your work surface and clothes before you start.

2. **Wooden spoon** for mixing grout with water/paint.

3. **Mixing container** for mixing grout with water/paint.

4. **Water** is added to grout powder to form a paste. Water is also used to dilute PVA adhesive.

5. **Acrylic paint** for colouring grout.

6. **Tweezers** for positioning small tile shapes.

7. **MDF board** can be used as a base for mosaic.

8. **Terracotta dish and flower pot** are some of the items that can be transformed with mosaic.

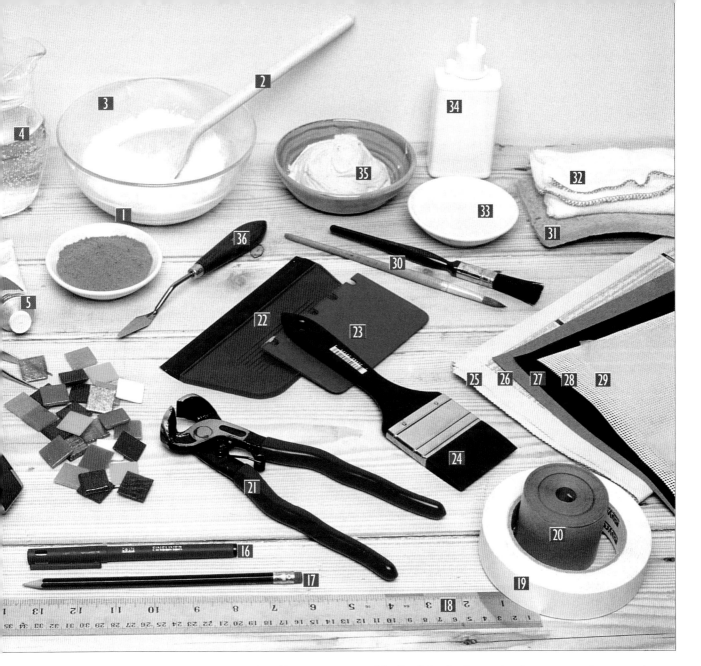

9. **Goggles** must be worn when cutting tiles.

10. **Hammer** for smashing tiles.

11. **Dust mask** must be worn when mixing grout.

12. **Rubber gloves** must be worn when working with grout.

13. **Wax candle** is used for the indirect mosaic technique (see pages 42–47) to prevent the brown paper from sticking to the board.

14. **Scissors** for cutting out designs and masking tape.

15. **Craft knife** for cutting brown parcel paper when using the indirect technique.

16. **Fibre-tipped pen** for drawing shapes on to glass and glazed ceramic tiles.

17. **Pencil** for transferring designs and for marking shapes on to ceramic tiles. A chinagraph pencil may be used on glass tiles.

18. **Ruler** for drawing straight lines.

19. **Masking tape** for securing designs and for masking areas from grout.

Materials and equipment

Continued from page 7

20. **Gummed paper tape** for stretching brown parcel paper when using the indirect technique.

21. **Art Mosaic professional tile nippers** for cutting and shaping tiles.

22. **Grout spreader** for spreading grout.

23. **Notched spreader** for applying tile adhesive.

24. **Colour shaper (wide)** for spreading grout over small areas.

25. **Newspaper** for covering a work surface when using grout.

26. **Brown parcel paper** is used as a temporary base for the mosaic in the indirect technique.

27. **Carbon paper** for transferring designs.

28. **Tapestry mesh** can be used as a base for mosaic (see page 39).

29. **Clear plastic bag** to contain tile pieces when they are smashed with a hammer.

30. **Paintbrushes** A large brush is used to apply diluted PVA adhesive when sealing a surface. A small brush is used to apply wallpaper paste to tiles (indirect technique).

31. **Sponge** for cleaning away excess grout.

32. **Cloth** for final polishing after grouting.

33. **Wallpaper paste** is used to stick tiles temporarily to brown paper in the indirect technique.

34. **PVA adhesive** for sticking mosaic tiles in place on certain surfaces such as wood, MDF, terracotta and tapestry mesh. Diluted PVA can be used to seal surfaces.

35. **Art Mosaic professional mosaic tile adhesive** for securing tiles to walls and objects such as terracotta pots.

36. **Palette knife** for applying tile adhesive.

Tiles and decoration

Mosaic may be created using a variety of materials. Here are just a few ideas. There are no set rules – you may choose just one type of tile, or decide to combine several different ones within the same piece.

> **Note** The tile quantities suggested at the start of each project are rough estimates and include a wastage allowance of between thirty and fifty per cent, depending upon how much cutting/shaping is involved.

Art Mosaic glass tiles These are industrially-manufactured and are available in a good selection of colours. They are uniform in size – approximately 2cm (¾in) square. The smooth, flat surface is designed as the face. The back of each tile has bevelled edges and a ridged underside to aid good adhesion. As with paints, the price often varies depending upon the shade.

Ceramic mosaic tiles There are several different types available. For this book, we have chosen a range of natural shades with a matt surface. These are excellent for creating Roman-style pieces. Unlike the glass tiles, they are the same front and back.

Ceramic household tiles These often form the starting point for a first mosaic and are ideal for 'crazy paving' projects (see pages 34–37). Tile shops sometimes offer seconds at a reduced rate. The tiles can be smashed using a hammer to make random shapes, or cut using tile nippers to make more precise ones.

Broken crockery Scour jumble sales and junk shops for decorative plates and cups etcetera. Again, smash at random using a hammer or carefully crunch away with tile nippers to cut out individual motifs.

Beads, pebbles and shells The inclusion of small objects such as these within a mosaic can be very effective.

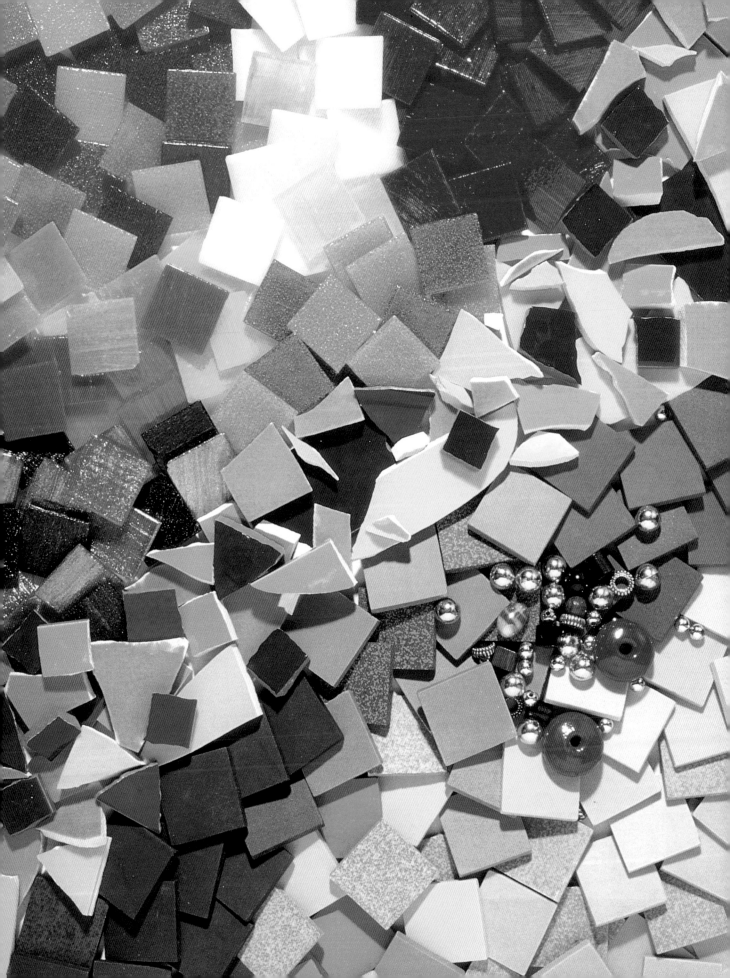

Aztec mirror frame

Transferring a design, gluing and grouting

This mirror project is ideal for a first mosaic. We have kept the design simple and have used only two colours. As the mosaic involves no cutting of tiles, this piece can be completed relatively quickly!

Try adapting the grid pattern provided to vary the design. You can also adjust the colours to suit your own interior décor (see page 48).

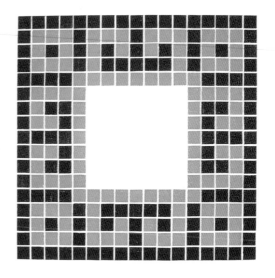

You will need

- Mirror tile, 15cm (6in) square
- 4 self-adhesive pads
- MDF board, 9mm (³⁄₈in) thick, 37cm (14½in) square
- Glass mosaic tiles: 128 royal blue, 112 mid sky blue
- PVA adhesive and paintbrush
- Scrap paper
- Carbon paper, pencil, ruler and scissors
- Masking tape
- Tile grout (white)
- Grouting equipment: wooden spoon, mixing container, jug of water, rubber gloves, dust mask, grout spreader, sponge and cloths

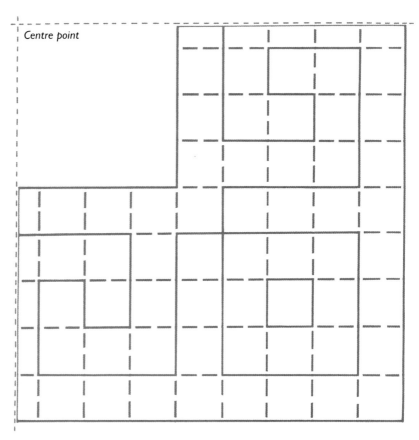

Centre point

Pattern for the Aztec mirror frame

Enlarge on a photocopier by 175% for a full-size design.

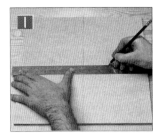

1. Use a pencil and ruler to divide the MDF board into quarters.

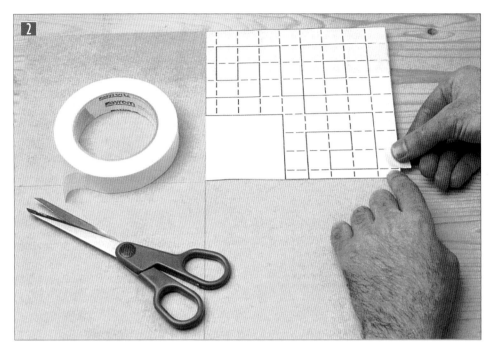

2. Enlarge the design on a photocopier to fit one quarter of the board. Secure one edge of the photocopy in position with masking tape.

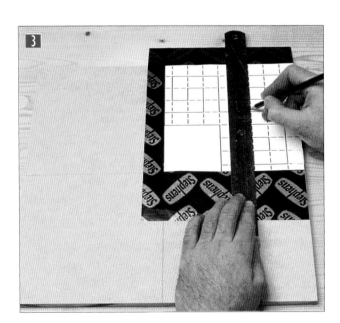

3. Slide a piece of carbon paper face down underneath and trace over the design using a pencil and ruler.

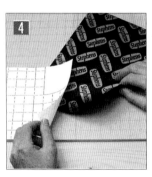

4. Repeat the process three more times until all four quarters are complete.

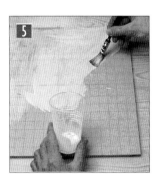

5. Mix a small quantity of PVA adhesive with an equal amount of water. Use a paintbrush to apply a coat to the upper surface of the MDF board to seal it. Leave to dry for approximately thirty minutes.

Aztec mirror frame

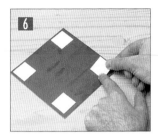

6. Attach four self-adhesive pads to the back of the mirror tile and position it in the centre of the board.

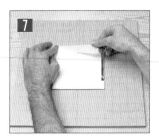

7. To protect the mirror whilst you are working, cover it with a square of scrap paper secured with masking tape.

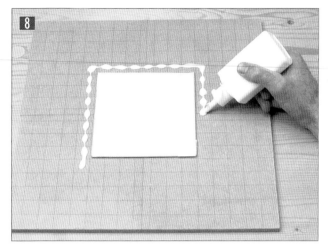

8. Apply beads of PVA adhesive around the edge of the mirror.

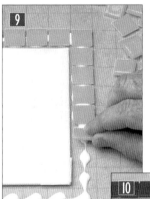

9. Position mid sky blue tiles around the mirror to create the inner border. Make sure the tiles are placed ridge-side down. Leave approximately 2mm ($^1/_{16}$in) between each tile.

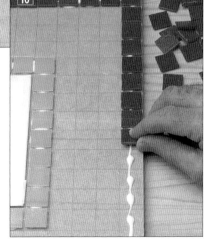

10. Following the same procedure, complete the outer border using royal blue tiles. Ensure tiles do not overlap the edges of the board.

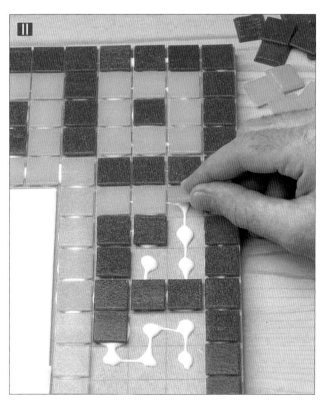

11. Now complete the remainder of the pattern using both colours. Leave to dry overnight.

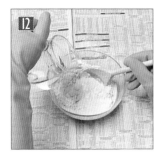

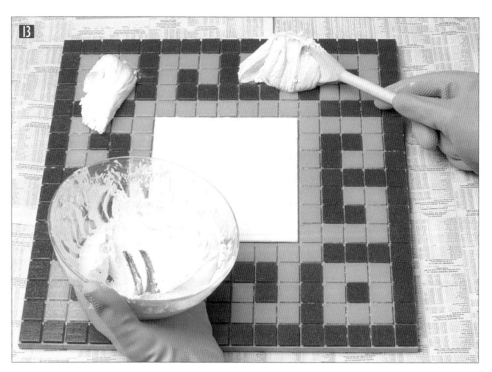

12. Cover your work surface with newspaper and put on rubber gloves and a dust mask. Place grout powder in a mixing container and gradually add water, stirring continuously, until a smooth, thick paste is achieved.

13. Spoon the grout mixture directly on to the surface of the mosaic.

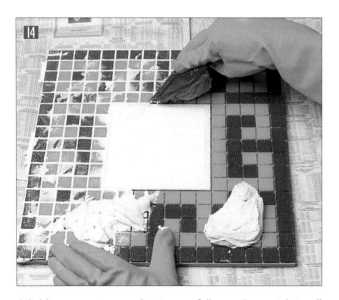

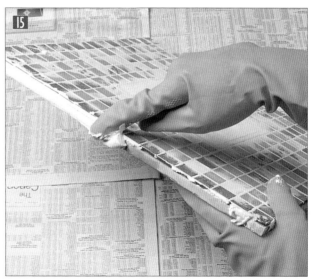

14. Use a grout spreader to carefully work grout into all the gaps between the tiles. Spread the grout in different directions to ensure that every crevice is filled.

15. Apply grout all around the outer edge of the board using your finger.

Aztec mirror frame

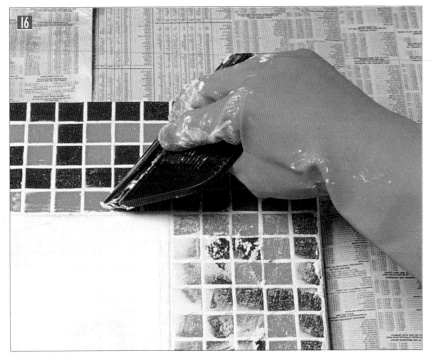

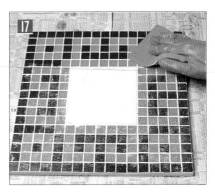

17. Clean the surface using a damp sponge.

16. Scrape away all excess grout with the spreader. Leave to dry for approximately ten minutes.

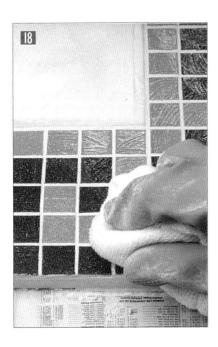

18. Polish with a dry cloth. Leave to dry overnight. Remove the paper from the mirror.

Note If your finished mosaic is to hang in a kitchen or bathroom, it is advisable to seal the back of the MDF board with a coat of paint or varnish to protect it from moisture.

Aztec mirror frame
This simple mirror is functional, attractive and easy to make. Glass tiles come in a good range of blues and greens – ideal for bathrooms.

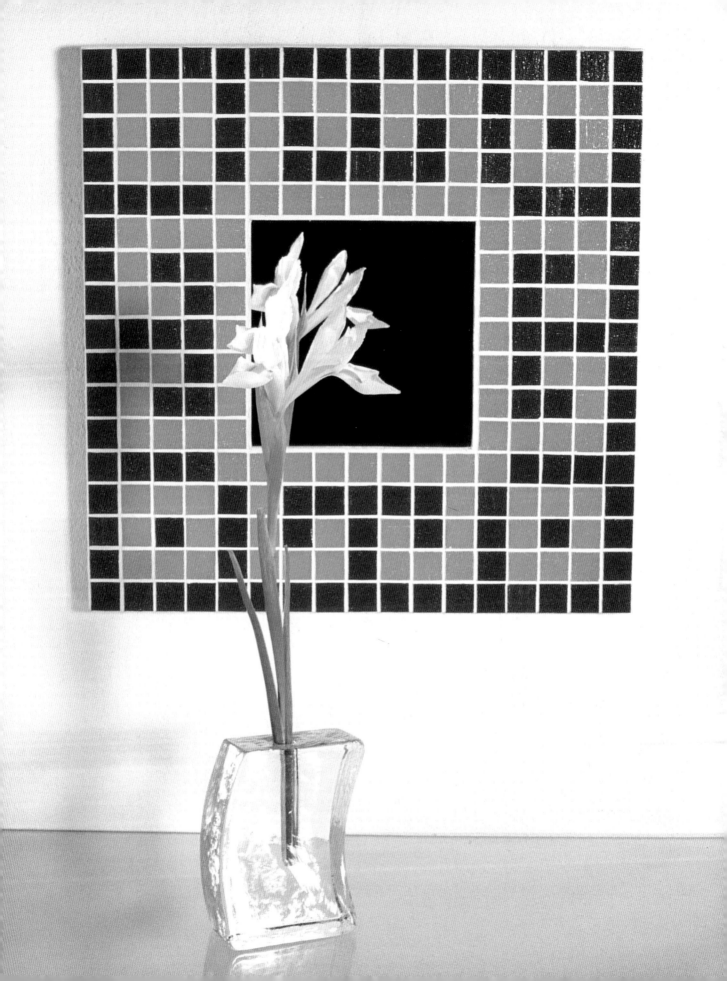

Kilim table

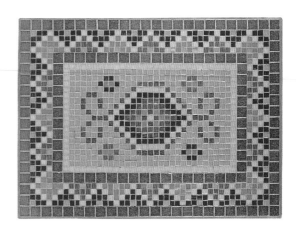

Cutting squares

This stunning table top was inspired by the pattern and colour of Persian textiles. The combined use of whole tiles and quarters provides a good introduction to cut mosaic. You will find that using quarter tiles enables greater detail to be expressed within a small area.

With a little practice, you will soon become proficient with tile nippers.

Note This geometric design may be adapted to fit an existing table base.

You will need

- MDF board, 12mm (½in) thick, 38.5 x 51.5cm (15 x 20¼in)
- Glass mosaic tiles: 170 deep aqua, 115 pale aqua, 80 poppy red, 40 deep orange, 40 pale orange, 90 pale beige
- Table base
- Tile nippers and goggles
- PVA adhesive and paintbrush
- Masking tape
- Carbon paper, pencil and ruler
- Tile grout (brown) and grouting equipment

Centre line

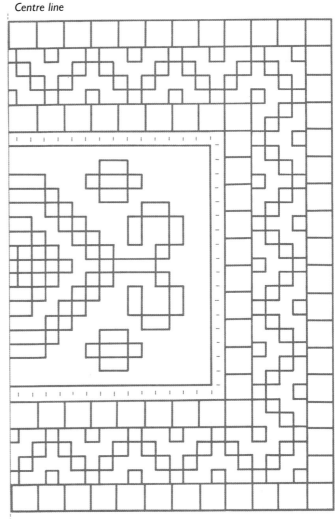

Pattern for the Kilim table

Enlarge on a photocopier by 290% for a full-size design.

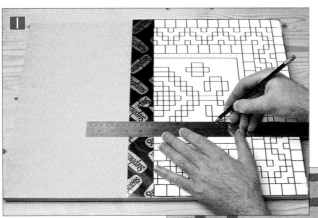

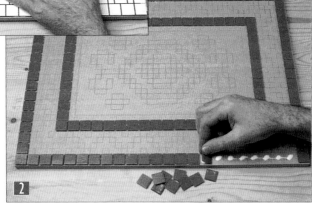

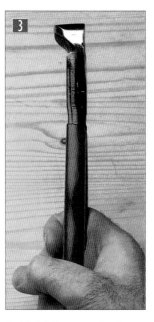

1. Use a pencil and ruler to divide the MDF board into two equal halves. Enlarge the design on a photocopier to fit one half of the board. Secure one edge of the photo-copy in position. Transfer the design using carbon paper (see page 11).

2. Seal the board with diluted PVA adhesive (see page 11). Apply beads of glue to the inner and outer borders, then press deep aqua tiles into place.

3. Hold the mosaic tile nippers towards the ends of their handles. If you are right-handed, make sure the curved edge of the cutting jaws is pointing to the left.

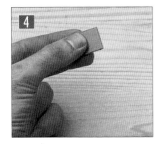

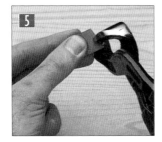

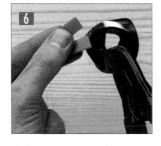

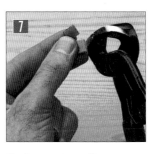

4. Support a pale aqua mosaic tile between the thumb and first two fingers of your other hand. Ensure the tile is held with the smooth side uppermost.

5. Insert the tile approximately 4mm ($\frac{1}{8}$in) into the nipper jaws.

6. Squeeze the nipper handles together. The tile should break across the centre into two roughly equal halves.

7. Cut each half in two to produce quarter tiles. Repeat this cutting procedure to create quarters of the other colours.

Kilim table

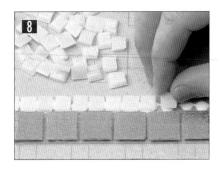

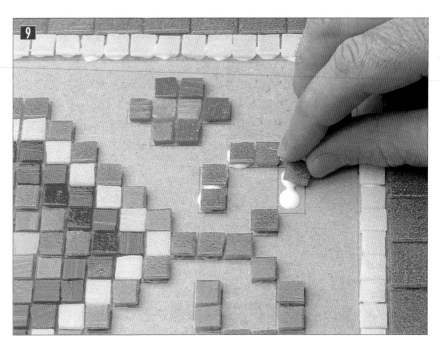

8. Apply beads of PVA adhesive inside the inner border. Press quarter tiles of pale beige into place.

9. Create the central motif using quarters of all the various shades except pale aqua. Stick down each piece individually using a small bead of PVA adhesive.

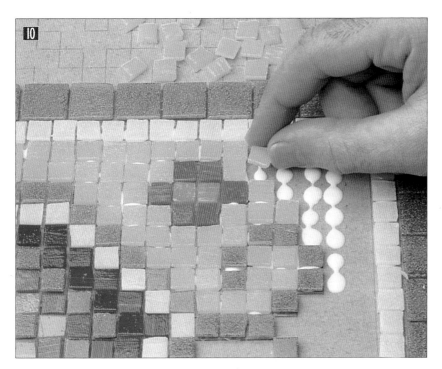

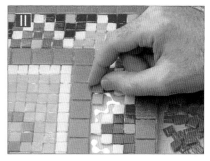

11. Complete the remaining border pattern using quarter tiles of colours as indicated. Leave to dry overnight. Attach the table top to a suitable base and then grout (see pages 13–14).

Kilim table

This table is made using a combination of whole and quartered glass mosaic tiles. Brown grout enhances the rich palette of colours used.

10. Following the same procedure, fill the central area using quarter tiles of pale aqua.

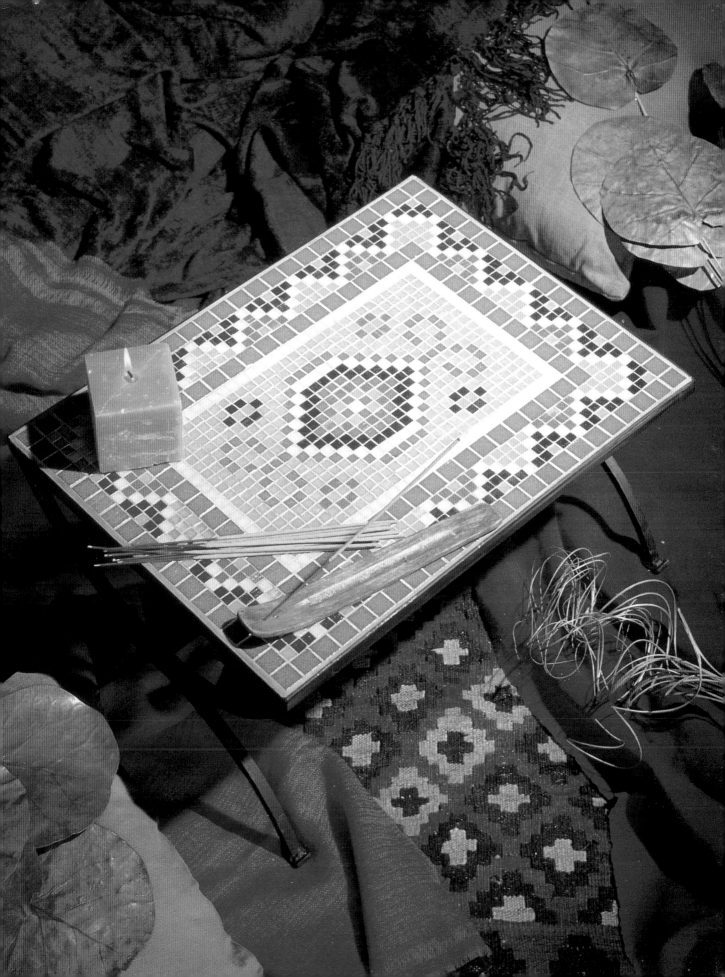

Seahorse panel

Cutting triangles and wedge shapes

The seahorse is always a popular image with students on our courses. In order to convey the detail of the creature in mosaic, you need to create more complex shapes using the tile nippers. Follow the photographs carefully to learn the cutting techniques. Do not worry if some tiles shatter during shaping. It is a good idea to keep any off-cuts, as they may well fit at a later stage.

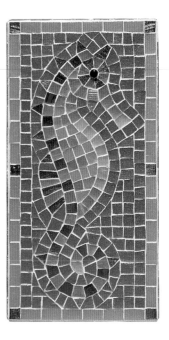

You will need

- MDF board, 9mm (³/₈in) thick, 28 × 14cm (11 × 5½in)
- Glass mosaic tiles: 30 candy pink, 10 amethyst, 15 copper gold, 90 sky blue, 80 mid sky blue
- Small dark bead
- Tile nippers and goggles
- Tweezers
- PVA adhesive and paintbrush
- Masking tape
- Carbon paper, pencil and ruler
- Fibre-tipped pen
- Tile grout (white) and grouting equipment

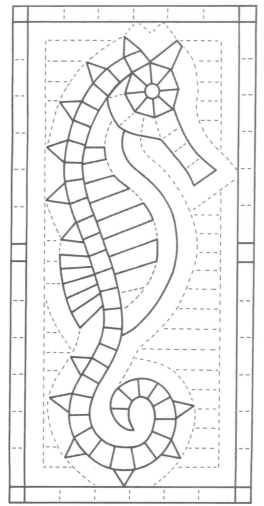

Pattern for the Seahorse panel

Enlarge on a photocopier by 215% for a full-size design.

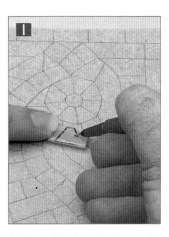

1. Transfer the design and seal the MDF board with diluted PVA adhesive. Create the eye from copper gold and candy pink wedge shapes. Begin by copying the eight wedge shapes on to half tiles using a fibre-tipped pen.

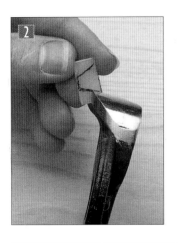

2. Cut along the drawn pen lines. Remember the tile will fracture in the direction of the nipper jaws.

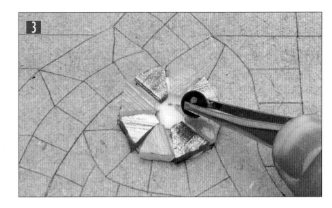

3. Position the wedge shapes in a circle around the eye and stick in place with PVA adhesive. Complete the eye by gluing a bead in the centre.

4. Use a combination of quarters and wedge shapes to outline the seahorse's body. Alternate pink and amethyst shades down the back and tail. Use pink for the chest and head.

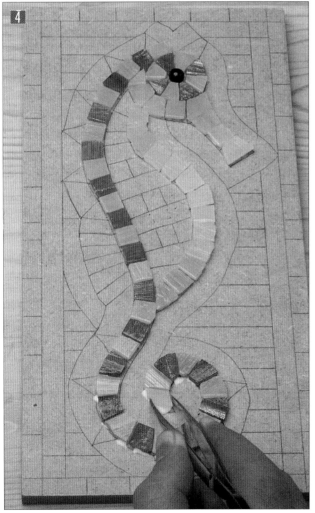

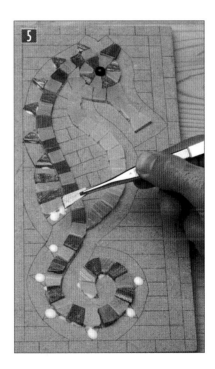

5. Cut triangles of copper and position them to form the spine. Use long wedge shapes of copper and pink for the fin.

Seahorse panel

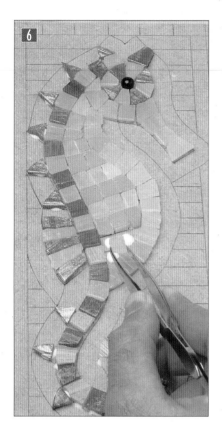

6. Fill the body area using rows of pink and mid sky blue. Shape quarters to fit.

7. Outline the completed seahorse and inner border using sky blue. Fill the rest of the background in the same colour.

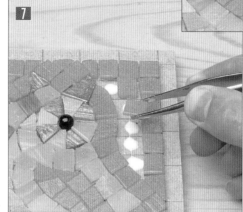

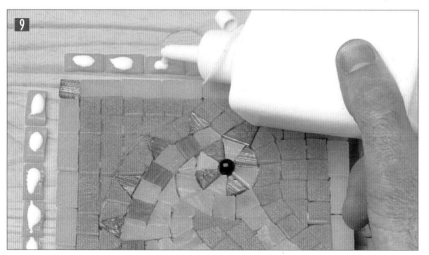

8. Cut thirty-six halves of mid sky blue and six quarters of copper. Stick in place to form the outer border. Make sure that the cut edges face inwards and the smooth bevelled edges outwards.

9. Cut forty-two halves of mid sky blue. Lay them face (smooth side) down around the board, ensuring the cut edges face inwards. Add a small blob of PVA adhesive to each tile half. Leave for around ten minutes until tacky.

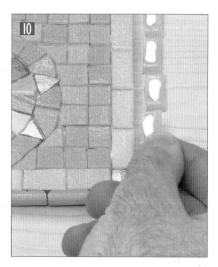

10. Press the side pieces firmly into place all around the board. Leave to dry overnight. Grout and finish.

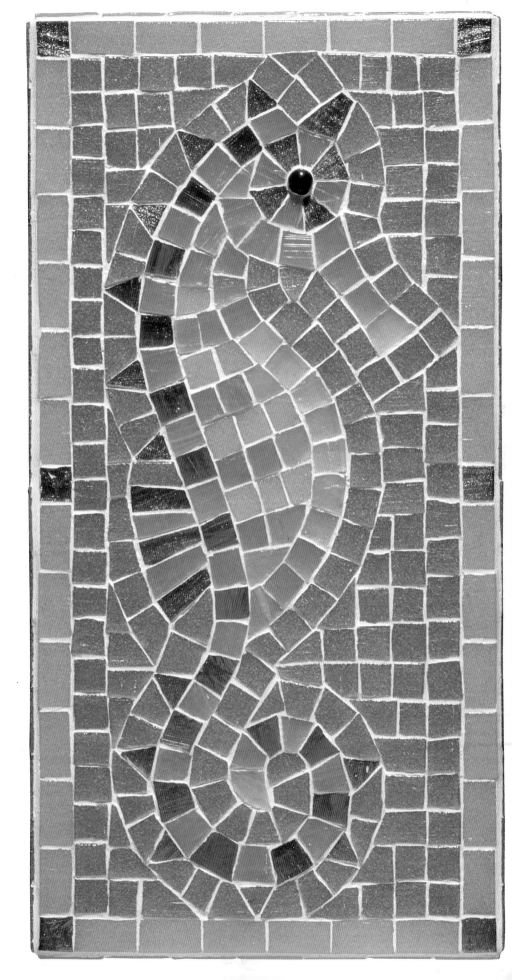

Seahorse panel

The semi-transparent and iridescent qualities of glass mosaic tiles make them ideal for underwater subjects. The blues of this panel work well with the soft pinks and gold of the seahorse. If you choose an alternative colour palette, ensure there is enough contrast between the seahorse and the background.

Orange tree dish

Cutting circles and leaf shapes

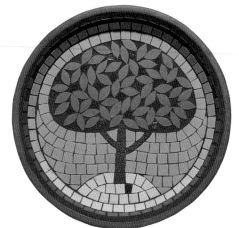

This decorative piece may be placed on a horizontal surface or displayed on a wall, using a plate hanger. The design incorporates large gaps between the leaves and the fruit in the tree. The terracotta grout introduces another colour to the mosaic and works well with the clay of the dish itself. Do not feel you have to stick to the design exactly. Leaves and oranges may be placed at random to create the desired effect.

You will need

- Unglazed terracotta dish (with a flat surface), 21cm (8¼in) in diameter
- Glass mosaic tiles: 10 deep orange
- Ceramic mosaic tiles: 50 green, 50 mustard, 50 blue, 40 yellow, 10 speckled brown
- Tile nippers and goggles
- PVA adhesive and paintbrush
- Carbon paper, pencil and scissors
- Masking tape
- Tweezers
- Tile grout (terracotta) and grouting equipment

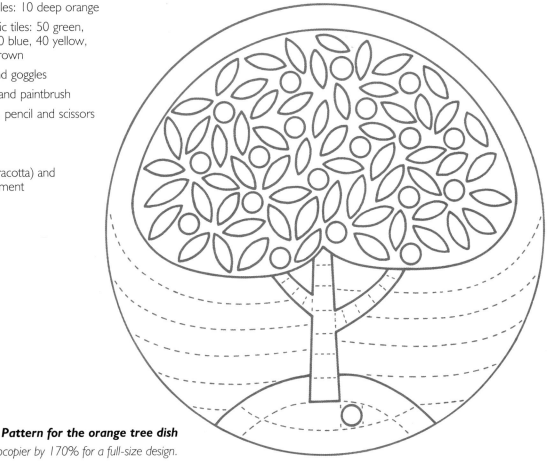

Pattern for the orange tree dish

Enlarge on a photocopier by 170% for a full-size design.

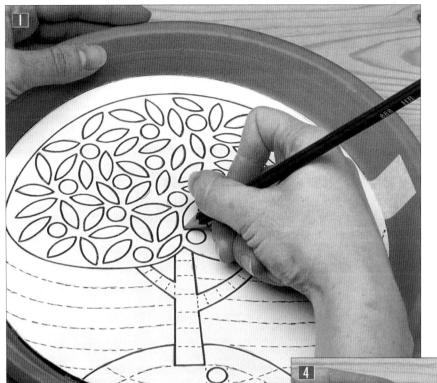

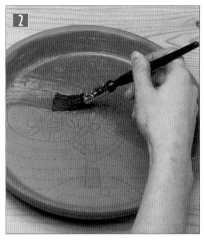

2. Seal the surface of the dish by painting on a coat of diluted PVA adhesive.

1. Enlarge the design on a photocopier to fit the flat surface of your terracotta dish. Cut it out and transfer the design on to the dish using carbon paper.

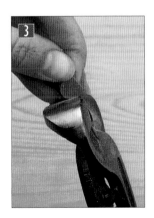

3. Cut the orange glass tiles into quarters and then nibble away the corners to form small circles.

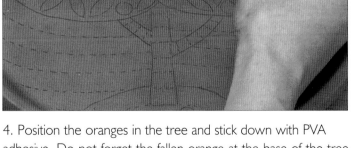

4. Position the oranges in the tree and stick down with PVA adhesive. Do not forget the fallen orange at the base of the tree.

Orange tree dish

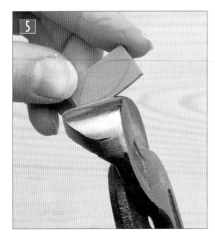

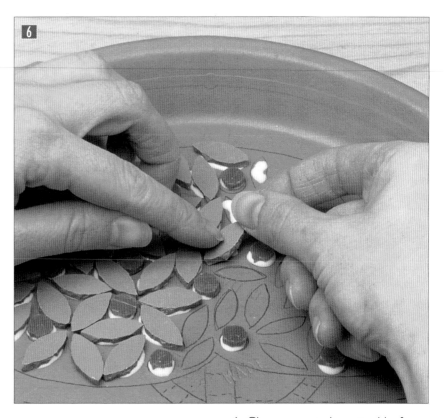

5. Cut green and mustard ceramic tiles in half. Use a pencil to draw on the leaf motifs then cut to shape.

Note You can use a pencil to mark shapes on to ceramic tiles. Use a fibre-tipped pen or chinagraph pencil for glass tiles.

6. Glue green and mustard leaf shapes in place around the oranges.

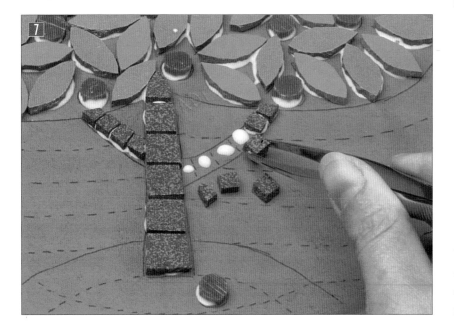

7. Use a line of speckled brown quarters for the tree trunk. Cut quarters into four tiny squares to make the branches.

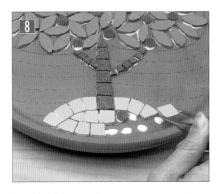

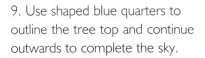

8. Combine yellow squares and wedge shapes to form the hill.

9. Use shaped blue quarters to outline the tree top and continue outwards to complete the sky.

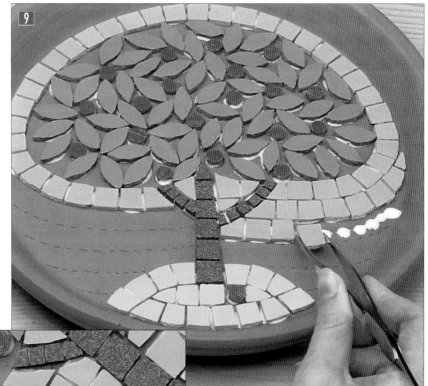

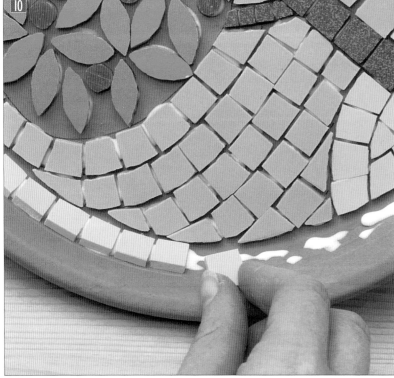

10. Attach a row of yellow quarters around the side wall of the dish.

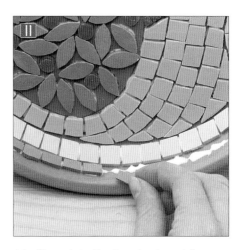

11. Complete the border by adding an outer row of alternating green and mustard tiles – use quarters cut in half. Leave to dry overnight.

Orange tree dish

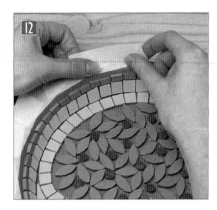

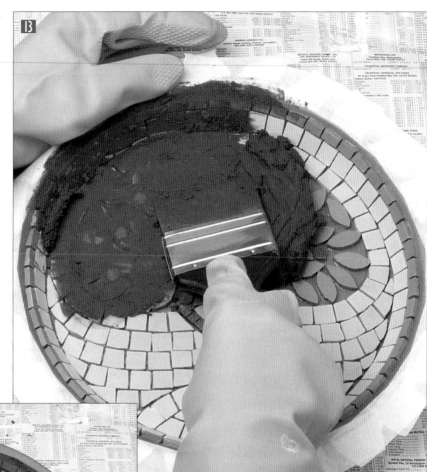

12. Apply short lengths of masking tape around the rim of the dish to protect it.

13. Spread terracotta grout over the entire surface of the dish. Use a colour shaper or narrow grout spreader to work the mixture into the flat base and up the side walls.

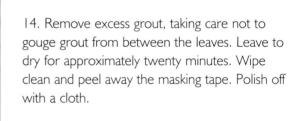

14. Remove excess grout, taking care not to gouge grout from between the leaves. Leave to dry for approximately twenty minutes. Wipe clean and peel away the masking tape. Polish off with a cloth.

Orange tree dish

Do not be afraid of using a variety of materials within the same piece. The combination of different shapes and reflective qualities adds interest to this dish – the natural hues of the matt ceramic contrast well with the vibrant orange glass.

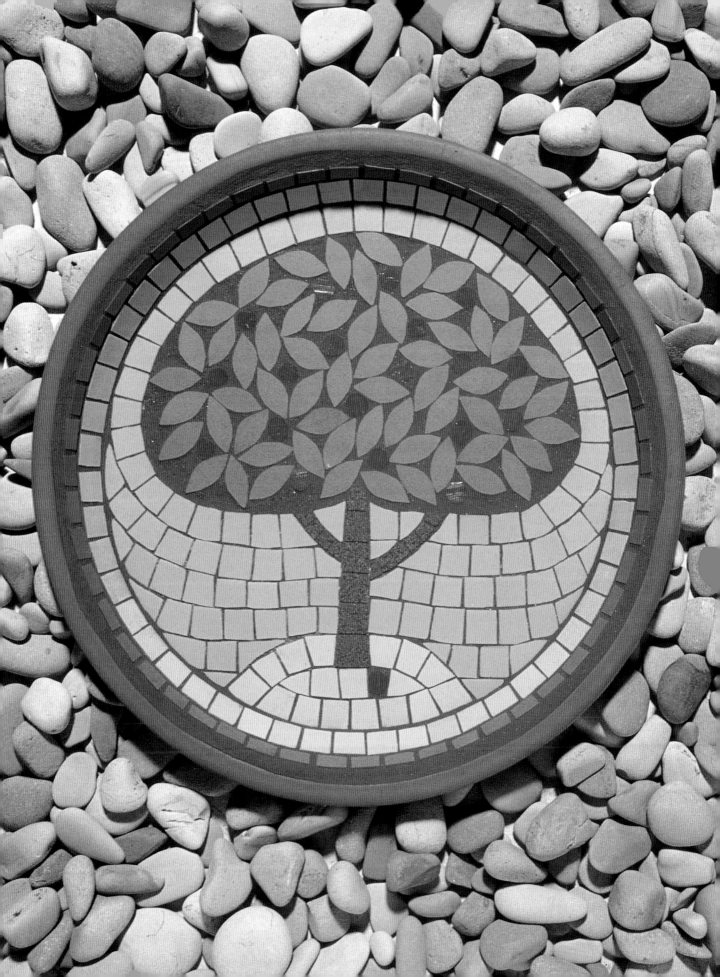

Jewelled clock

Incorporating beads and colouring grout

This ornate clock is embellished with gold beads and framed with brass edging strip (available from model shops). In this project the grout is coloured using blue acrylic paint. As in the Orange Tree Dish, the areas of grout form an integral part of the design.

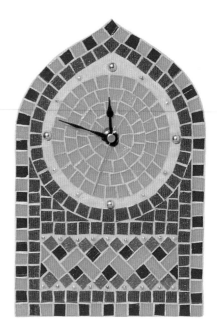

> **Note** Clock mechanisms are available from craft suppliers and specialist shops. Make sure that the hands are the correct size and style for your clock face.

You will need

- MDF board, 9mm (³⁄₈in) thick, 16.5 x 25cm (6½ x 10in)
- Glass mosaic tiles: 15 poppy red, 50 mid sky blue, 50 royal blue, 5 dark sky blue
- 4 large and 26 small gold beads
- Brass edging strip 12mm (½in) in width, small brass tacks and hammer
- Clock mechanism and hands
- Wood saw
- Drill with 10mm (³⁄₈in) bit
- Tile nippers and goggles
- Tweezers
- Fibre-tipped pen
- PVA adhesive and paintbrush
- Carbon paper, pencil and ruler
- Masking tape
- Acrylic paint: blue
- Tile grout (white) and grouting equipment

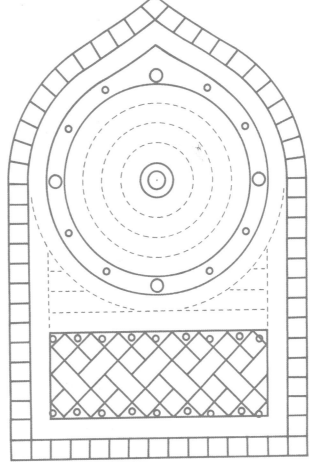

Pattern for the jewelled clock

Enlarge on a photocopier by 200% for a full-size design.

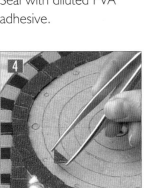

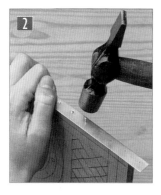

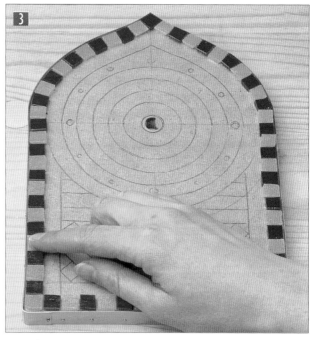

1. Transfer the design on to MDF board and saw to shape. Drill a 10mm ($^3/_8$in) hole in the centre for the clock mechanism. Seal with diluted PVA adhesive.

2. Punch or drill small holes in the brass edging and then tack it around the edges of the board.

3. Cut poppy red and mid sky blue quarters. Starting at the top, stick them in place to form the outer border. Alternate the colours as you work.

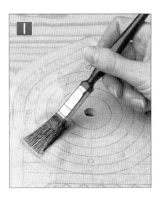

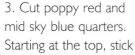

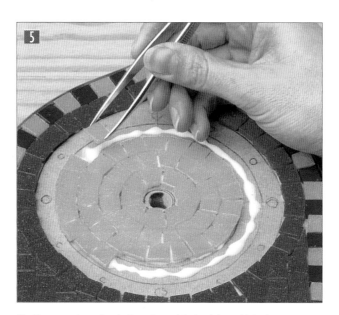

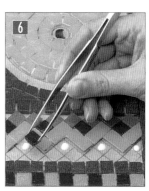

4. Use quarters of royal blue to map out the circumference of the clock face and the border of the panel underneath. Use triangles and quarters to fill in the remaining gaps.

5. Create the clock face in mid sky blue. Work outwards from the centre using wedge shapes. Remember to leave a hole for the clock collar.

6 Cut halves, quarters and small triangles of dark sky blue, poppy red and mid sky blue. Use these to form the decorative panel below the clock face.

Jewelled clock

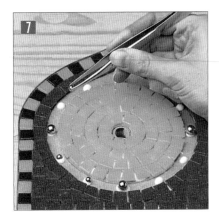

7. Stick four large gold beads in place to mark the quarter hours. Use the smaller beads for the other hours and to fill in the spaces in the panel below.

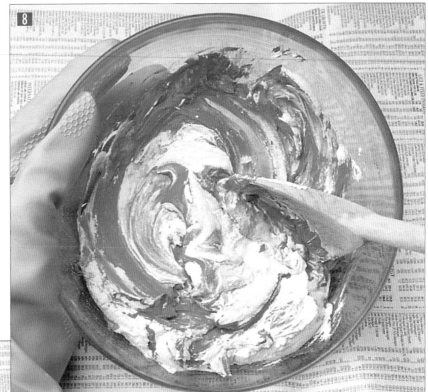

8. Mix white grout powder to a thick creamy paste (see page 13). Add acrylic paint to colour it as required, and stir well. Remember the grout will dry lighter in colour.

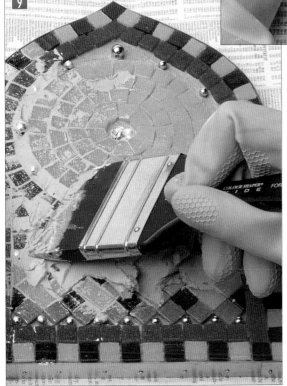

9. Stuff a little newspaper into the central hole and then grout the clock panel. Leave for twenty minutes. Wipe the surface clean, ensuring the area around the beads is level with the surrounding tiles. Leave to dry overnight.

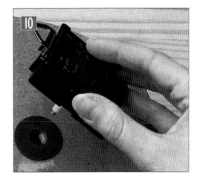

10. Attach the clock mechanism and hands, following the manufacturer's instructions.

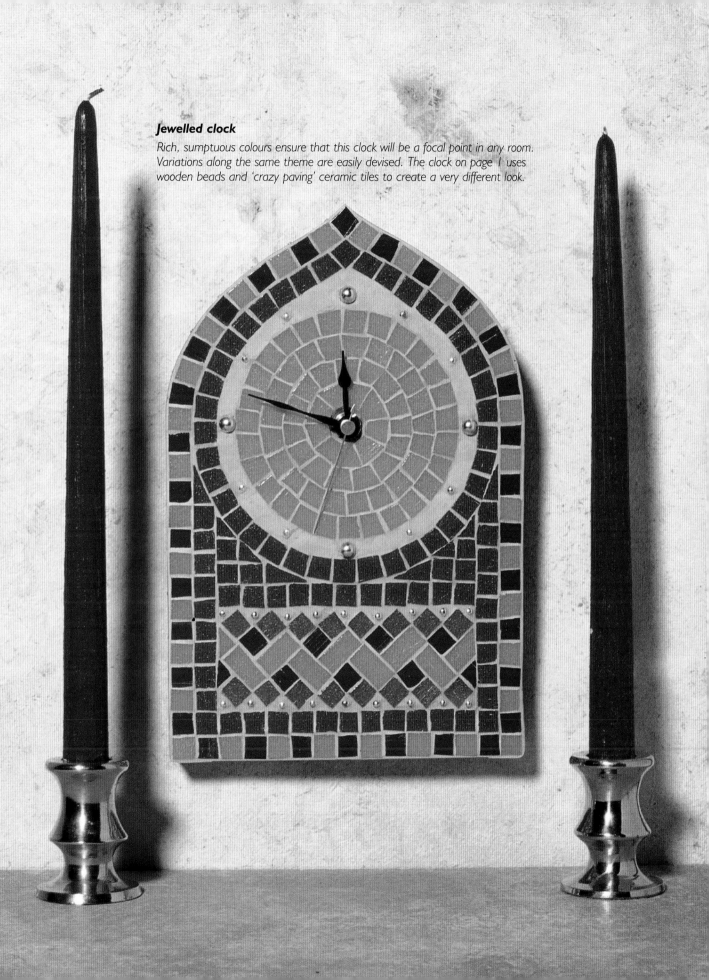

Jewelled clock

Rich, sumptuous colours ensure that this clock will be a focal point in any room. Variations along the same theme are easily devised. The clock on page 1 uses wooden beads and 'crazy paving' ceramic tiles to create a very different look.

Crazy plant pot

Using broken tiles

Household tiles are ideal for this project. They are usually fairly cheap and readily available. You could also use broken crockery, pebbles or even shells. This decorative plant pot uses a combination of controlled shapes for the borders and the leaf motif, with 'crazy paving' for the background.

This technique is very versatile and often used to cover larger surface areas such as garden furniture and the exteriors of whole buildings.

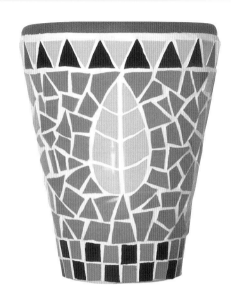

Note This pot is suitable for outdoor use but it is susceptible to frost damage. You may choose to bring it indoors during winter. Check the manufacturer's recommendations for adhesive and grout usage.

It is advisable to seal the inside of the pot with a coat of varnish before you add soil and plants.

You will need

- Terracotta pot, approximately 18cm (7in) tall
- Ceramic bathroom tiles: lime green, indigo, orange, jade green
- Hammer
- Strong clear plastic bag
- Tile nippers and goggles
- Tile adhesive
- Palette knife
- PVA adhesive and paintbrush
- Pencil and scissors
- Fibre-tipped pen
- Tile grout (white) and grouting equipment

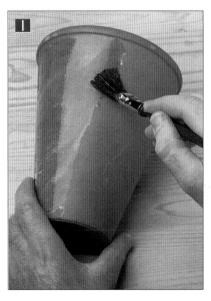

1. Seal the outer surface of the terracotta pot using diluted PVA adhesive. Allow to dry thoroughly.

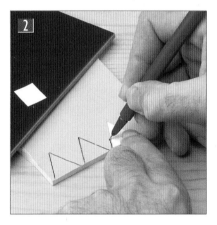

2. Cut simple square and triangle templates from paper. Place each template on a tile and draw around the shape with a fibre-tipped pen. Draw triangles on lime green and indigo. Mark squares on jade green and indigo.

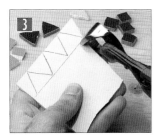

3. Following the lines, cut out the shapes using tile nippers.

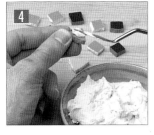

4. Use a palette knife to 'butter' each piece individually with tile adhesive.

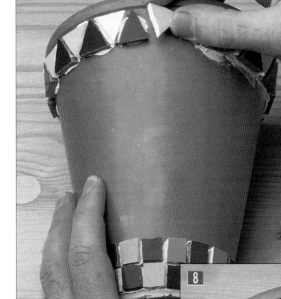

5. Apply jade green and indigo squares to the bottom border. Use lime green and indigo triangles to form the top border. Press each piece gently into position.

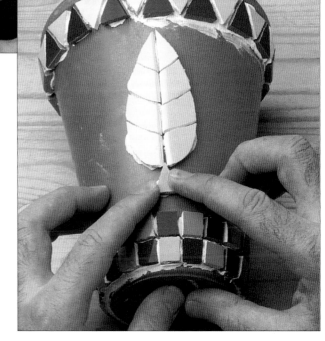

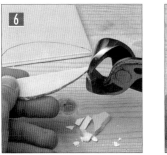

6. Mark out and cut two leaf halves from a lime green tile. To minimize cutting, use the straight edge of the tile for the straight side of each piece.

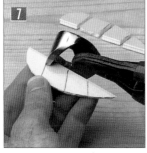

7. Divide each leaf half into sections then cut along the pen line using tile nippers. Cut a small jade green triangle for the stem.

8. Apply tile adhesive to the centre of the pot then position the leaf shapes and the triangular stem.

35

Crazy plant pot

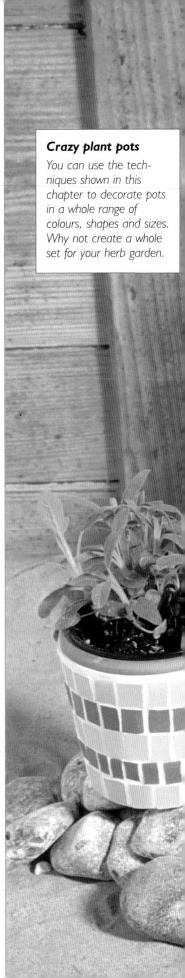

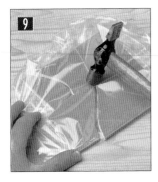

9. Place a whole orange tile in a clear plastic bag. Hit it with a hammer several times to create random pieces for the background.

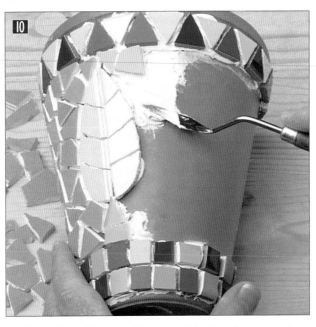

10. Spread small areas of the pot with tile adhesive and attach the broken fragments in a crazy paving pattern. Some pieces will still need trimming with the tile nippers to fit. Leave overnight for the tile adhesive to set.

Crazy plant pots

You can use the techniques shown in this chapter to decorate pots in a whole range of colours, shapes and sizes. Why not create a whole set for your herb garden.

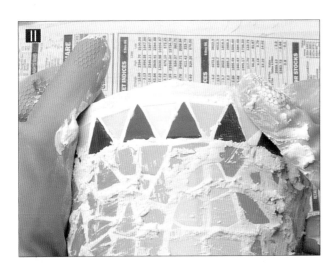

11. Stick masking tape around the top rim. Use a grout spreader to apply grout to the body of the pot, and your fingers for around the rim and the base. (Be careful of sharp edges!) Leave for twenty minutes.

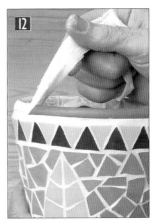

12. Wipe away excess grout with a damp sponge. Remove the masking tape, then polish clean.

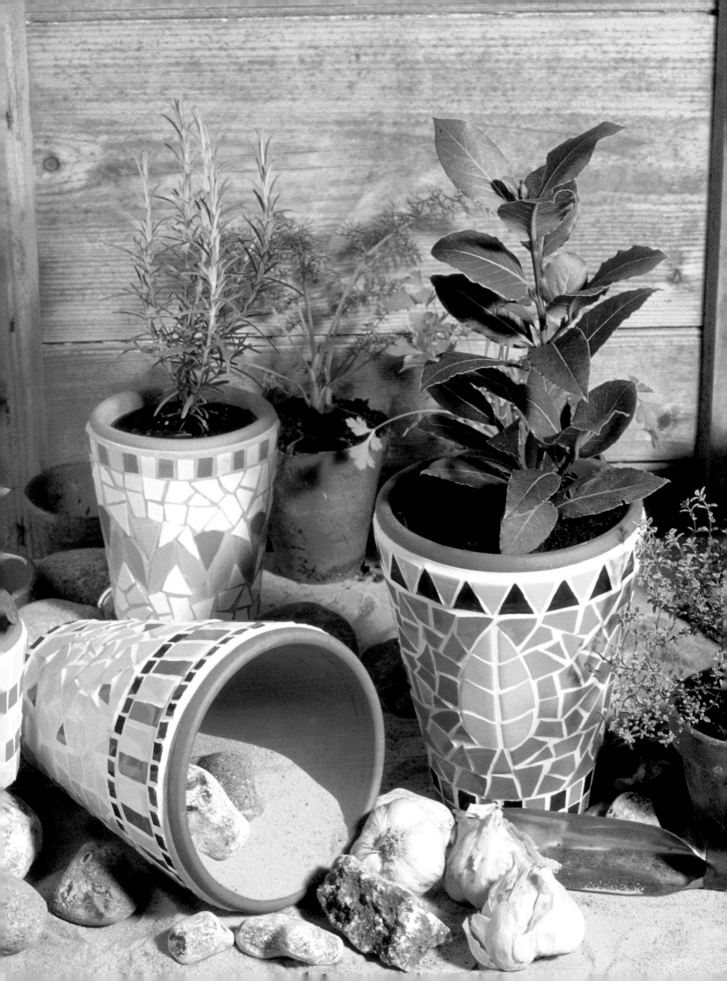

Pepper tile

Using a mesh base

Cut mosaic tends to be a rather time-consuming craft. However, you do not always need to cover large areas . . . just a small section can make a bold statement!

Working on mesh allows the mosaic to be constructed on a horizontal surface before being positioned vertically on a wall. A set of inserts may be used to break up an expanse of plain tiles to great effect.

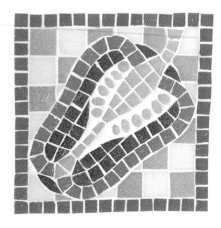

> **Note** This pattern is intended to work with commercial 15.25cm (6in) wall tiles, but designs can be adapted to match your own tile size.

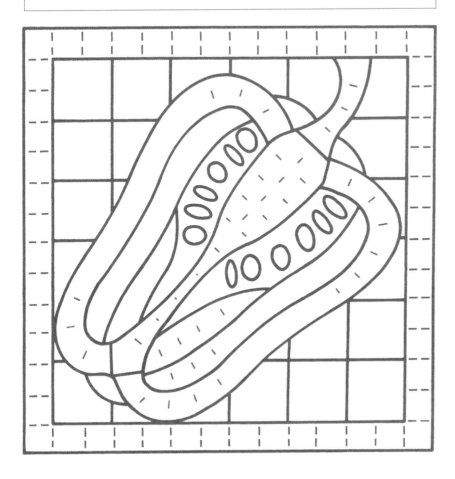

You will need

- Tapestry mesh
- Small board (wood/MDF)
- Glass mosaic tiles: 20 pale orange, 10 yellow, 10 pale beige, 20 opaque white, 20 pale sky blue, 10 spring green, 10 emerald green
- Tile nippers and goggles
- Tile adhesive
- Clear plastic bag
- PVA adhesive and paintbrush
- Masking tape
- Fibre-tipped pen
- Scissors
- Notched spreader
- Tile grout and grouting equipment

Pattern for the pepper tile

Enlarge on a photocopier by 135% for a full-size design.

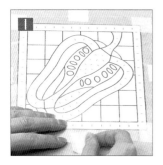

1. Photocopy the design to size and tape it to a board. Cover with a square cut from a clear plastic bag and secure with masking tape. (This will prevent the mesh from sticking to the paper.)

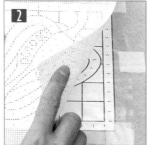

2. Cut a square of tapestry mesh slightly larger than the design. Place it on top of the plastic and tape it down.

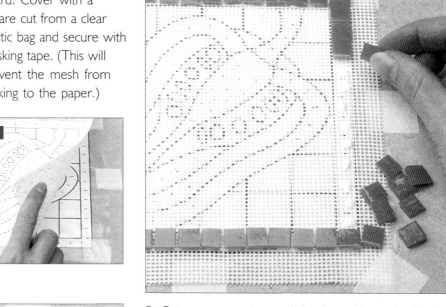

3. Cut orange quarters and glue in position using PVA adhesive to form the tile border.

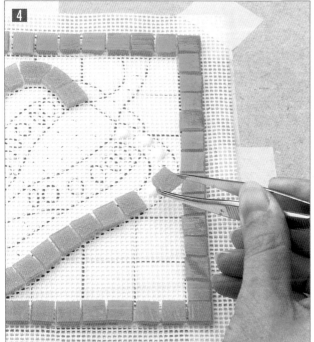

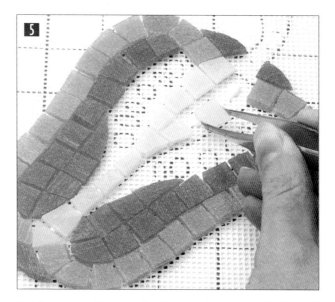

4. Cut quarters and wedge shapes from the spring green tiles and use these to outline the pepper.

5. Use emerald green for the top, bottom and sides of the pepper and use pale beige up the centre.

Pepper tile

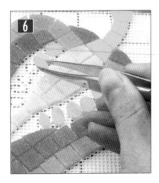

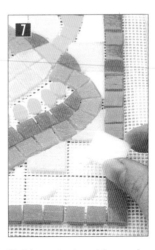

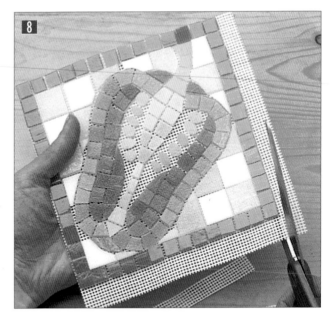

6. Use a fibre-tipped pen to draw shapes for the stalk and seeds on to yellow quarter tiles. Cut to size then glue into position.

7. Use whole white and sky blue tiles to form the chequerboard background. Some will require careful shaping to fit around the pepper. Leave to dry overnight.

8. Gently peel the mosaic-covered mesh from the plastic. Trim away the excess tapestry mesh with scissors.

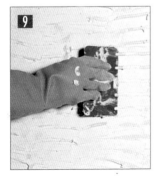

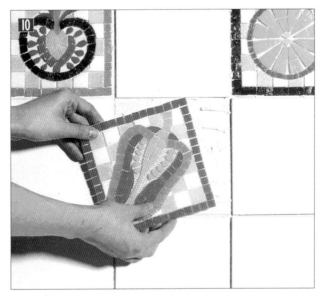

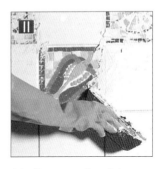

9. Apply an even coat of tile adhesive to the wall using a notched spreader.

10. Position plain tiles and mosaic inserts on the tile adhesive and press gently into place. Leave to dry overnight.

11. Grout and polish clean the whole area in the usual way.

Pepper tile

The inclusion of mosaic borders or motifs can transform the whole look of a surface. Mosaic tile inserts can be positioned in isolation or in small groups as shown here.

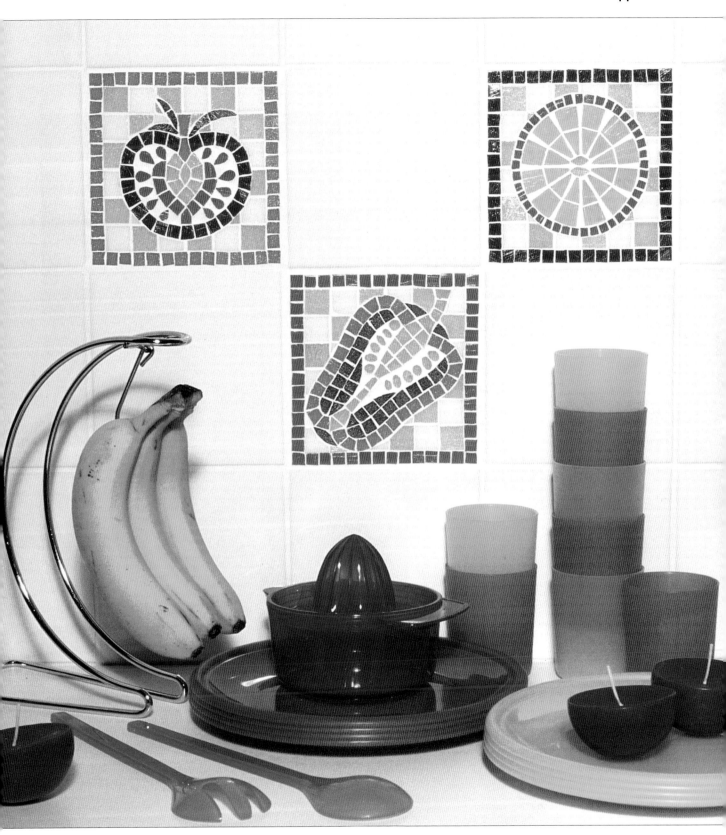

Fancy fish panel

Indirect technique

The indirect technique enables a mosaic to be constructed off-site and later installed in position. It is a two-stage process used to create a uniform, flat surface. Firstly, the tiles are stuck face-down on to brown paper using a temporary adhesive such as wallpaper paste. The whole sheet of mosaic is then pressed into a bed of tile adhesive. Finally, the paper is peeled away to reveal the face of the mosaic for the very first time!

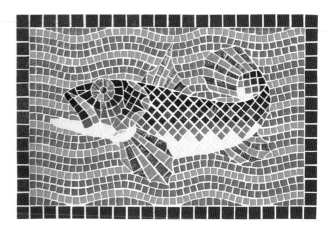

You will need

- Board (MDF/wood) 12mm (½in) thick, approximately 60 x 45cm (23½ x 17¾in)
- Scrap wood
- Brown parcel paper
- Wax (candle)
- Gummed paper tape
- Masking tape
- Carbon paper, pencil and scissors
- Wallpaper paste/paper adhesive
- Small paintbrush
- Glass mosaic tiles: 75 royal blue, 200 sky blue, 100 mid sky blue, 25 white, 20 pale orange, 30 deep orange, 10 candy pink, 40 warm red, 3 black, 50 copper gold, 50 sand
- Tile nippers and goggles
- Fibre-tipped pen
- Craft knife
- Tile adhesive
- Tile grout (white) and grouting equipment

Note Remember that when you use the indirect technique, the finished mosaic will be the mirror image of your design. This is particularly important if you want to create a piece which features numbers or lettering.

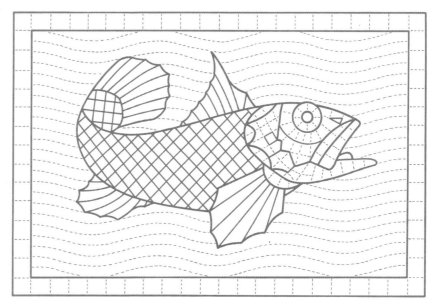

Pattern for the Fancy fish panel
Enlarge on a photocopier by 305% for a full-size design.

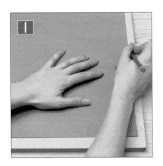

1. Cut a piece of brown parcel paper 52 x 36cm (20½ x 14in). Place it centrally on the board and then draw round the edge with a pencil.

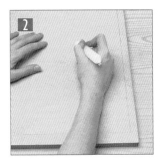

2. Scribble on the board within the pencilled rectangle using a wax candle. This will prevent the brown paper from sticking to the board.

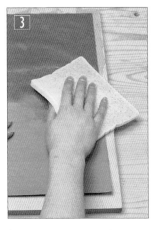

3. Place the paper back on the board and soak thoroughly with a wet sponge.

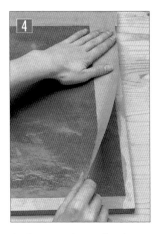

4. Secure along all edges using moistened gummed paper tape. Leave overnight for the paper to dry and become taut.

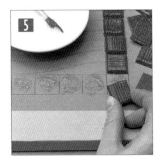

5. Transfer the photocopied design using carbon paper. Brush a little wallpaper paste along the outside border. Apply whole royal blue tiles. Continue to complete the border.

Note As this is the indirect method, all tiles must be stuck face (flat side) down.

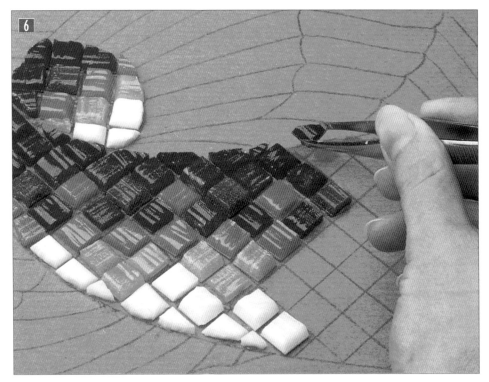

6. Fill in the fish's body using quarters of warm red, deep orange, pale orange, white and royal blue. Use triangles at the edges of the body.

Fancy fish panel

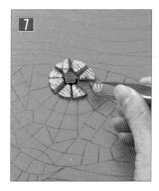

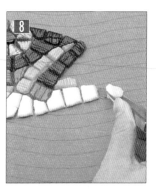

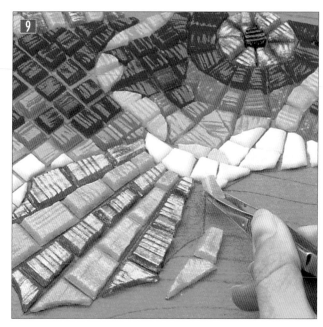

7. Cut a black circle and copper wedge shapes to create the eye.

8. Now work on the head. Mark difficult shapes on the tile using a fibre-tipped pen before cutting.

9. Create the fins using various shapes of copper and sand. Work in alternating stripes of colour.

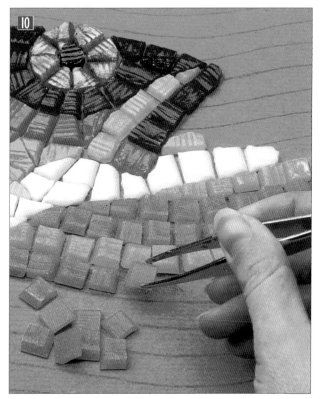

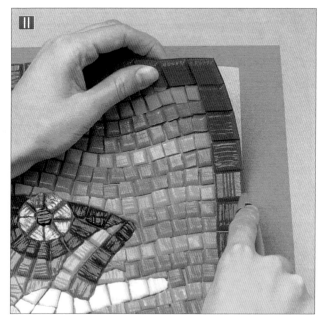

10. Form the wavy lines of the sea using quarters of sky blue and mid sky blue. Leave to dry overnight.

11. Use a craft knife to cut along the edge of the mosaic and remove it from the board.

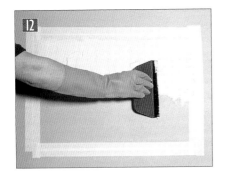

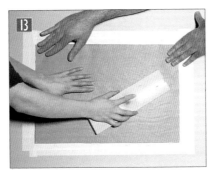

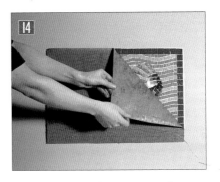

12. Use masking tape to outline the area of wall where the mosaic is to be positioned. This should be the exact size of your mosaic panel. Use a spreader to apply a thin layer of tile adhesive to the wall, within the taped boundary.

Note Ensure the wall surface is sound and free from dust and grease before you begin.

13. Place the mosaic paper face towards you on to the adhesive bed and press down gently using a flat piece of wood. An extra pair of hands will come in useful here! Remove the masking tape and leave to dry overnight.

14. Sponge the brown parcel paper backing with warm water and allow it to soak in for ten minutes. (This will start to dissolve the wallpaper paste.) Gently peel back the paper to reveal the face of the mosaic.

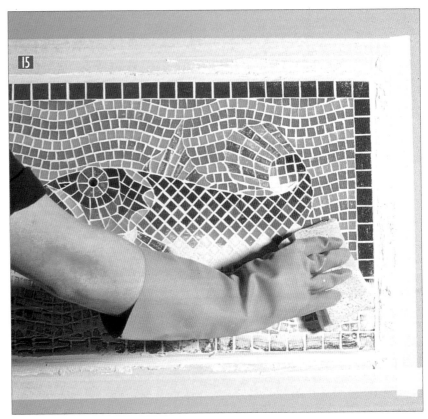

15. Wipe over the surface with a damp sponge to remove any glue residue. Apply masking tape to the wall leaving a 0.5cm (¼in) space around the mosaic. Grout the surface (see page 13), carefully bridging the gap around the edge using your finger. Finally, polish clean and remove the masking tape.

Fancy fish panel

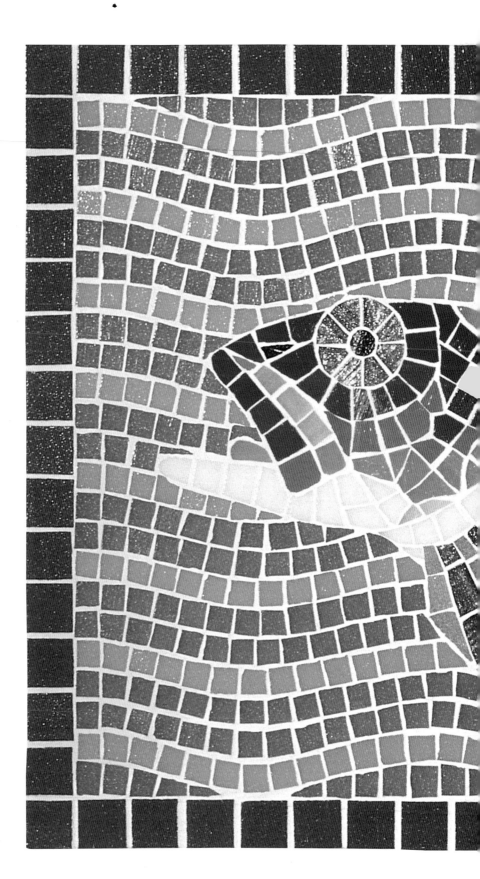

Fancy fish panel

This fish would look splendid as a splash-back or above a bath. Notice how the tiles have been positioned diagonally on the body to represent scales. The wavy two-tone background suggests the movement of water.

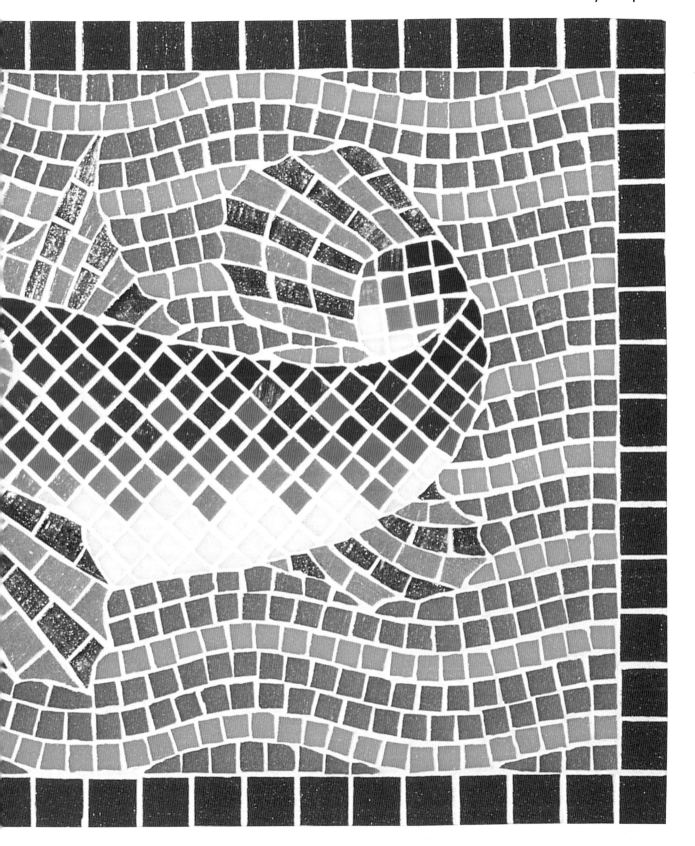

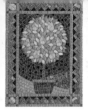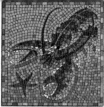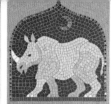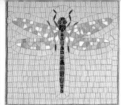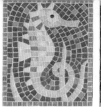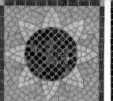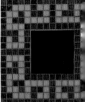

Index

beads 8, 21, 30, 32
brown parcel paper 8, 42, 43, 45

carbon paper 8, 11, 17
chinagraph pencil 7
clock 1, 30–33
cloth 8, 14
colour shaper 8
craft knife 7, 44
crazy paving 8, 34–37
crockery 8, 34

design, transferring a 7, 8, 11
dish 24–29
dust mask 6, 13

fibre-tipped pen 7, 20

goggles 6, 7, 17
grout 6, 7, 8
  colouring 6, 30, 32
  mixing 6, 13
grouting 6, 8, 13–14, 28, 32,
  36, 45
grout spreader 8, 13
gummed paper tape 8, 43

hammer 7, 8, 36

indirect technique 7, 8, 42–47

masking tape 7, 11
MDF board 6, 11, 17, 20, 43
mirror frame 10–15, 48
mixing container 6, 13

newspaper 8, 11
notched spreader 8, 40

paint, acrylic 6
paintbrush 8, 11
palette knife 8
panel 20–23, 42–47
pebbles 8, 34
pencil 7, 11, 17
plant pot 34–37
plastic bag 8, 36, 39
polishing 8, 14
PVA adhesive 6, 8, 11

rubber gloves 6, 7, 13
ruler 7, 11, 17

scissors 7
shells 8, 34
smalti 4
sponge 8, 14, 43, 45

surfaces, sealing 8, 11, 14, 25

table 16–19
tapestry mesh 8, 38, 39, 40
tesserae 4
tiles
  cutting 6, 7, 8, 16, 17, 20, 21,
    25, 35
  gluing 12, 22
  marking 7, 26, 34
  smashing 7, 8, 36
  types of
    ceramic 8
    commercial 38–41
    glass 8
    household ceramic 8, 34
tile adhesive 8, 35, 36, 40, 42, 45
tile nippers 8, 17
tile quantities 8
trencadis 4
tweezers 6

wallpaper paste 8, 42, 43
water 6
wax candle 7, 43
wooden spoon 6

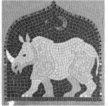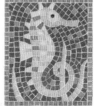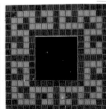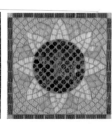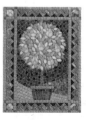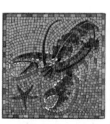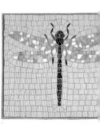